SUMMARY

On March 17, 2011, 1 month after the beginning of the Libyan revolution and up to 2,000 civilians dead, the United Nations Security Council (UNSC) decided to back a no-fly zone over Libya and authorized "all necessary measures" to protect civilians. While France, Great Britain, and the United States took immediate military action using air and missile strikes, considerations to hand the mission to the North Atlantic Treaty Organization (NATO) emerged within days of the operation. On March 22, 2012, NATO agreed to enforce the arms embargo against Libya; 2 days later, it announced it would take over all military aspects of UNSC Resolution (UNSCR) 1973. On March 31, 2012, Operation UNIFIED PROTECTOR (OUP) began. For the first time in its history, NATO was at war with an Arab country.

OUP turned out to be one of NATO's shorter, and seemingly also less controversial, missions. Mandated by both the League of Arab States and the UN as the regime of Colonel Muammar Qaddafi was launching assaults on peacefully demonstrating citizens, the mission had the aim to protect civilians from the air and sea. OUP has thus been described as a success — a success NATO badly needed after its decade-long engagement in Afghanistan. However, the Libyan operation was not without its critics. Described as a "war of choice" rather than a "war of necessity," it achieved its goals more by accident than by design, according to some commentators. Yet, the operation also exposed strategic shortcomings, which are analyzed in this monograph.

First, in the public appraisal of the operation, air power was seen as the crucial element in winning the conflict. This view is only partially correct; just as air power works best when integrated with land forces, NATO's operation was, in part, decided by those forces engaged with the Libyan regime's forces—although both forces were not truly integrated. Nevertheless, overestimating the impact of air power can mislead decisionmakers in future conflict.

Second, the operation exposed some flaws in NATO's command structure, which was under reform when the conflict erupted. Joint Force Command Naples (JFC-Naples), in charge of the operation, was not properly equipped for an actual crisis of this dimension, but managed to improvise on a large scale.

Third, the Alliance paid very little attention to Libya's cultural terrain. They had no cultural advisers on the staff of OUP—no one from Libya nor from any other Arab country. Also, there was no one who was familiar with the local conditions. The improvised advice OUP relied on turned out to be a failure; as officers involved in the campaign admitted, nobody predicted several of the turns the operation took. Given that the ground component was crucial to the mission's success, cultural advice would have made an important contribution to the general understanding of the situation within Libya as the operation evolved.

Fourth, there was some disconnect between the legal and the political solution of the crisis. As the legal interpretations of UNSCR 1973 made clear, the operation did not seek to topple Qaddafi's regime, let alone assassinate him. Its sole aim was the protection of civilians in a situation of internal conflict, and therefore it conformed to the norm of "Responsibility to Protect"; yet, against the backdrop of international political pressure, the Alliance's neutrality and its agenda quickly became a point of discussion.

Fifth, the Libyan regime's strategic communication proved to be a lot more resilient and creative than NATO's strategic communication. It succeeded not only in recruiting a public relations firm for this purpose, but managed to escort BBC journalists into a hospital showing corpses of young children supposedly killed in NATO air strikes.

Last, but not least, the aftermath of NATO's Libya operation was not planned at all, as the Libyan National Transitional Council firmly rejected any military personnel on the ground, even UN observers. As the regime's security forces had virtually imploded, Libya's security therefore fell into the hands of the multiple militias, which continued to proliferate after the conflict had ended.

The euphoria over the end of a brutal regime, which lasted 4 decades in Libya, should not disguise the fact that the consequences of OUP are not yet fully visible. It would be a mistake to think that NATO's Libya adventure ended with the drawdown of the military mission; whether the Alliance likes it or not, its reputation is at stake in Libya's long reconstruction process.

THE NORTH ATLANTIC TREATY ORGANIZATION AND LIBYA: REVIEWING OPERATION UNIFIED PROTECTOR

When demonstrators took to the streets of Tunis in January 2011, Libya's de facto head of state Colonel Muammar Qaddafi appeared on state TV. He declared he was "in pain" about the removal of Tunisia President Ben Ali, and described the demonstrators as "led astray" by Wikileaks cables written "by Ambassadors to create chaos."[1] His appearance expressed his concern, as that of many other dictators in the region, about a similar fate. Yet, it took another month and the toppling of Egypt's President Mubarak for Libyans to engage in similar demonstrations, which began on February 16 in the Eastern city of Benghazi and quickly spread to other parts of the country.[2] Confronting police and armed forces, the civilian death toll rose dramatically within a few days.[3] In a degree of violence surpassing that of its neighboring states by far, Libya's security forces were accused of savagely attacking unarmed civilians.

Qaddafi himself appeared on TV, calling on his supporters to hunt the "greasy rats" on drugs, "the dirt," as he described the demonstrators.[4] Within days, Libya's diplomatic staff at the United Nations (UN), the League of Arab States, as well as numerous other missions, resigned out of protest against the regime's actions against civilians. Two weeks into the events, U.S. President Barack Obama called for Qaddafi's resignation, while the International Criminal Court announced investigations into crimes against humanity committed by Qaddafi and his inner circle. While first calls for a no-fly zone emerged following the regime's use of its air force against the protesters, France's foreign minister Alain Juppe rejected such a move as:

France, for its part, does not think that in the current circumstances military intervention, NATO forces, would be welcomed in the south of the Mediterranean and could be counterproductive.[5]

As the regime continued to crumble among high-level defections, the self-proclaimed body representing the Libyan rebels, the National Transitional Council, called for the implementation of a no-fly zone as the clashes between government and rebel forces reached new and violent dimensions.[6] The League of Arab States, which had already suspended Libyan membership 3 weeks earlier, supported this call.[7] While regime forces marched onto the rebel city of Benghazi, Qaddafi declared that his forces would "show no mercy, and no pity" to the rebels.[8] The next day, March 17, 2011, a month after the beginning of the Libyan revolution and up to 2,000 civilians dead, the UN Security Council (UNSC) decided to back a no-fly zone over Libya and authorized "all necessary measures" to protect civilians.[9] While France, Great Britain, and the United States took immediate military action using air and missile strikes, considerations to hand over to the North Atlantic Treaty Organization (NATO) emerged within days of the operation. On March 22, 2012, NATO agreed to enforce the arms embargo against Libya; 2 days later, it announced it would take over all military aspects of the UNSC 1973.[10] On March 31, 2012, Operation UNIFIED PROTECTOR (OUP) began. For the first time in its history, NATO was at war with an Arab country.

OUP turned out to be one of NATO's shorter, and seemingly also less controversial, missions. Mandated by both the League of Arab States and the UN as the regime of Colonel Qaddafi was launching assaults on peacefully demonstrating citizens, OUP had an aim to protect civilians from the air and sea. As the operation came to an end after 204 days and 26,323 sorties (including 9,658 strike sorties),[11] 3,124 vessels in the Mediterranean had been captured, Colonel Qaddafi's regime had been toppled, and many civilian lives had probably been saved. OUP has thus been described as a success—a success NATO badly needed after its decade-long engagement in Afghanistan. However, the Libyan operation was not without its critics. Described as a "war of choice" rather than a "war of necessity," OUP achieved its goals more by accident than by design, according to some commentators.[12] The operation quickly highlighted tactical shortcomings, such as the lack of targets in a mission conducted solely from the air and sea, and made the need for improved intelligence sharing within the Alliance apparent. Yet, the operation also exposed strategic shortcomings that will be analyzed here.

Overall, a balanced assessment of OUP's impact will have to take into account Libya's still uncertain future development and the impact of the crisis on regional security. As NATO has ceased all involvement in Libya as of October 31, 2011, it has not taken any role in the country's post-conflict stabilization efforts. At the time of this writing, Libya was stable, yet showed increasing signs of instability, particularly in the security sector. Should Libya implode, this would have repercussions not only for future operations and post-conflict planning, but in particular for NATO's potential involvement in out-of-area crises.

There are, by and large, six lessons the Alliance can draw from its Libya operation. These regard air power, its command structure, the understanding of culture, the interpretation of UNSC Resolution 1973, strategic communication, and NATO's relations with the region in general.

Lesson 1: Do Not Draw the Wrong Conclusions Regarding Air Power.

OUP gave the impression to some commentators of being a "clean" conflict conducted solely from the air and sea, as specified by UNSC Resolution 1973 in the requirement that there be no "foreign occupation force of any form."[13] The implementation of the resolution's three military elements—namely, the weapons embargo, the no-fly zone, as well as the "protection of civilians"—was therefore limited to air and naval power. Since the latter was largely used for the implementation of the maritime embargo, the decisive force used by NATO during the operation therefore was from the air. Two dimensions of the resolution were to be implemented from the air: the no-fly zone, of course, but also the protection of civilians—which was more vague than the other two military elements of the resolution and therefore offered more room for interpretation. This protection of civilians aspect was to become a point of contention later on.

Another point of discussion leading up to the operation was the question of kinetic action. For some Allies, such as Germany, military action in any form in Libya was simply not politically acceptable. For others, such as the United States, the extent of this action had legal implications. Since the U.S. President requires congressional approval to engage American forces in military action for longer than 60 days without a declaration of war according to the War Powers Resolution of 1973, the White House argued that the Libyan operation was not a war.

4

U.S. military operations are distinct from the kind of 'hostilities' contemplated by the Resolution's 60-day termination provision. U.S. forces are playing a constrained and supporting role in a multinational coalition. . . . U.S. operations do not involve sustained fighting or active exchanges of fire with hostile forces, nor do they involve the presence of U.S. ground troops, U.S. casualties or a serious threat thereof, or any significant chance of escalation into a conflict characterized by those forces.[14]

Regardless of the interpretation of OUP's military action, a point of contention before the operation was the Libyan air defense system. As its destruction was considered decidedly kinetic, initial debates at the political level sought the implementation of a no-fly zone without any such action. The idea, however, was quickly abandoned, as it became clear that the Libyan regime would not only not respect such a no-fly zone (as Iraq had done more or less from 1991 to 2003), but respond in full force. As then-U.S. Secretary of Defense Robert Gates said:

Let's just call a spade a spade, a no-fly zone begins with an attack on Libya to destroy the air defenses. That's the way you do a no-fly zone. And then you can fly planes around the country and not worry about our guys being shot down. But that's the way it starts.[15]

In addition to the general political concern over the extent of the no-fly zone, there were also practical considerations, such as the large Libyan air space— which would be difficult to control—and the fact that Libyan helicopters would still be able to fly, since their use of low altitudes would make them more difficult to detect. This view was disputed by Air Force officers, who claimed not only that, given the limited number of helicopter staging areas in Libya, these would be easy to destroy, but also that Aim-9X Sidewinders, an air-to-air missile, could shoot them down easily.[16] As the political pressure mounted, the operational plan for OUP finally included the neutralization of the air defense system, a task largely taken on by the United States, particularly before the handover to NATO.

Before the conflict, the Libyan air defense system was considered one of the most robust air defense networks in Africa, second only to Egypt's. It included 31 long-range surface-to-air missile sites and 17 radar sites along the country's Mediterranean coast line, and was suspected to have been kept in shape after the U.S. attack in 1986 — as a retaliation to Libyan support of international terrorism. At that time, Libyan anti-aircraft fire set in only after the planes had entered Libyan airspace, but was heavy throughout the attack. One of 66 planes involved in the operation was lost.[17] Prior to the 2011 conflict, the location of the air defense system was identifiable, but "the condition and effectiveness of the communications, command and control network linking those sites has proven more difficult to determine."[18] Although it was assumed that Libya relied on outdated Soviet equipment and that its system would ultimately be less sophisticated than the Iraqi one, this remained a question mark before the actual conflict began. Ultimately, the destruction of the Libyan air defense system, mostly by the United States in the early days of the operation, was less difficult than General James Mattis, Commander of U.S. Central Command, had anticipated.[19] Within days, Admiral Samuel Locklear, Commander of the U.S. Naval Forces Europe, declared, "Gadhafi's long-range air defenses and his air force largely ineffective."[20]

Once the air defense system was largely neutralized, air power came to concentrate mostly on the government's command-and-control system. The protection of civilians—particularly in Benghazi, which was under immediate threat when the UN resolution was adopted—became paramount, but as the mission moved on it also became more complex. The intricacies of an internal conflict came to be particularly difficult as defecting soldiers of the Libyan military took ground vehicles with them, making it impossible to distinguish them from the air from actual regime forces. Several air strikes were reported in which rebel convoys were mistakenly hit by NATO, especially in the beginning of the operation.[21]

After the handover from Operation ODYSSEY DAWN (during which the United States was significantly involved) to OUP, about two-thirds of the strike sorties were shouldered by France and Great Britain, the rest by Italy, Canada, Denmark, Norway, Sweden (which is not a member of NATO), and Belgium.[22] The United Arab Emirates (UAE), Qatar, and Jordan, while participating with aircraft in the operation, remained in a supportive role.

NATO's air campaign over Libya has been largely described as a success—having achieved its objectives without any casualties. However, the understandably widespread, yet mistaken, conclusion was that this offered an effective demonstration of how warfare will be in the future, finally making it possible to circumvent the "zero tolerance" that Western societies profess for casualties. Yet, this reasoning revives the air power debate, exemplified by these two quotes:

Once the command of the air is obtained by one of the contended armies, the war must become a conflict between a seeing host and one that is blind.

H. G. Wells, *Anticipations of the Reaction of Mechanical and Scientific Progress upon Human Life*, 1902.

No aircraft ever took and held ground.

U.S. Marine Corps Manual

While the air power element in OUP was crucial, the war was not won from the air. Although NATO did not have boots on the ground, there were, indeed, ground troops: the Libyan rebel forces. Just as air power works best when integrated with land forces, NATO's operation was, in part, decided by those forces engaged with the Libyan regime's forces — although both forces were not truly integrated.[23]

Most analyses ignore the ground element of OUP, because it was not under NATO's operational control. Nevertheless, the armed elements more or less under orders of the Libyan National Transitional Council (NTC) indeed formed. These elements combined with those external actors who interpreted UNSC Resolution 1973 loosely, ground troops that not only fought the decisive battles but also encountered the highest battle losses. It is difficult to estimate the number of actual Libyan rebels — 250,000 registered with the Warrior Affairs Commission, an organization seeking their reintegration into civil society — although the commission itself admits that the number is very likely to be inflated by possibly 50 percent.[24] The same is true for casualties, which amount to 30,000, according to the Libyan health ministry, but do not differentiate between civilians, Qaddafi forces, or rebel fighters.[25]

The greater number of these fighters were, however, hardly militarily trained. Although basic military training was part of Libya's school curriculum, it did not constitute significant preparation for a situation of internal, and mostly urban, combat. As the average Libyan fighter was male, possessed an educational level at high school (27 percent) or elementary (35 percent), and was between 18 and 38 years old, there was in theory manpower available. In practice, however, there was virtually no command-and-control system, and basic military structures such as hierarchy, communication technology, and standard operating procedures were nonexistent.[26] As a result, concerns about these forces' capacity to gain and hold territory rose in the early days of the operation.

Since UNSC Resolution 1973 not only excluded a "foreign occupation force of any form" and also called on member states to "inform the Secretary General immediately of the measures they take" in order to protect civilians, there was room for maneuvering regarding foreign ground troops, but transparency was essential for the second.[27] The Panel of Experts established by the UN pursuant to UNSC Resolution 1973 thereby clearly indicated that "foreign military support, including deliveries of military materiel, had been crucial." In compliance with the transparency clause of the resolution, only four Member States—France, Italy, the United Kingdom (UK), and the United States—immediately notified the Committee of the intention to deliver the actual supply of military-related materiel or personnel to Libya.

This covered small teams of military advisors sent to Libya in order to support and advise on ways to organize (the NTC's) internal structure, manage its resources, and improve its communications.[28]

Although the exact size of these teams is classified, it is very likely to be limited to up to 20 personnel per country mentioned. Nevertheless, the sole presence of Western military personnel on Libyan ground was interpreted by a number of media outlets as a breach of UNSC Resolution 1973.[29] Rather than infringing on the issue of a foreign presence on the ground, however, these measures are questionable in terms of how they contribute to civilian protection.

In spite of the clause of the resolution pertaining to transparency, two states in particular did not notify the UN in time or adequately, namely, Qatar and the UAE. Upon inquiry by the panel regarding the transfer of weapons, military technology, and military personnel, the UAE replied that "NATO would be in a better position to answer those questions."[30] Similarly, Qatar originally did not inform the UN, but finally admitted to having sent a limited number of military personnel to provide military consultations to the revolutionaries, defend Libyan civilians, and protect air convoys, and that it had supplied those Qatari military personnel with limited arms and ammunitions for the purpose of self-defense.[31] Qatar also denied having provided the rebels with arms and ammunition.

This contradicts a statement by Qatar's Chief of Staff, Major General Hamad bin Ali al-Atiya, who declared "that the numbers of Qataris on the ground were hundreds in every region."[32] NTC chairman Mustafa Abdel-Jalil supported this by stating that the battles that ultimately led to victory were planned by Qatari officers, since the rebels were incapable of organizing professional forces. The presence of particularly Qatari military personnel on the ground highlights the blurred lines that existed during OUP.

Although in theory this was an operation to be conducted purely from the air and sea to protect civilians, in practice the difference between regime change and civilian protection, and between advice and military planning, became more unclear the longer the operation lasted.

In sum, the Libyan war indeed did possess a land component—one that was, however, not under NATO's command. Direct contact between the Alliance and the rebels was not possible, as it was not part of the mandate.

Coordinating with a crucial component that was only partly trained, unavailable for direct contact, and outside the command structure proved to be a challenge for JFC-Naples, which was in charge of the operation. Visualization of the situation on the ground was therefore improvised with all necessary means, including intelligence, media reports, and even a hotline established for Libyan civilians to call. Contradicting the official narrative, Qatar's Chief of Staff Major General Hamad bin Ali al-Atiya declared that it was the country's liaison officers in Naples who provided a link between NATO and the rebel forces. [33]

Lesson 2: Rethinking the JFC-Naples Structure.

OUP was run from JFC-Naples, which was at the time one of NATO's three operational commands (in addition to Joint Force Command Lisbon and Joint Force Command Brunssum). As OUP took the headquarters as much by surprise as by political leadership, the management of the operation allowed for a number of insights useful in the context of NATO's ongoing command structure reform. Overall, NATO's command structure has been downsized significantly since the end of the Cold War: in five revisions overall, it has shrunk from over five million active military and 78 headquarters to 3.8 million active military and 11 headquarters.[34] The ongoing reform of the command structure will reduce this number further.

The Alliance's integrated military command structure is not only unique (the Warsaw Pact, for instance, did not possess one), but is also considered one of its greatest assets. As a standing military structure that comprises personnel from all Allied nations, the structure allows for joint exercises, the establishment of interoperability, rules of procedures, and a quick response to crises. Created after the outbreak of the Korean War in 1950, the command structure was built along regional lines. Three regions (North, Center, and South) were headed by a Commander-in-Chief (CINC) who had control over regional air, land, and sea components.

In case of the Southern region, these were grouped under Allied Forces Southern Region (AFSOUTH), headed by CINC South, and initially all located in Italy — the Southern region originally did not include Greece and Turkey as they were not NATO members yet. AFSOUTH, whose headquarters was located in Naples, was to be responsible for "the integrated defence of the Southern European area (as well as) the Mediterranean."[35] This initial structure underwent a number of changes due to political disagreements as well as other changes: the accession of Turkey and Greece, later Spain, expanded the Mediterranean dimension, whereas the departure of France from the integrated military demanded restructuring.

AFSOUTH, the predecessor of JFC-Naples, was initially responsible for only the part of the Mediterranean that ranges from the West to a line in the Adriatic from Trieste to the Tunisian waters. The full

Mediterranean became its area of responsibility only with the admission of Turkey and Greece in 1952. Yet, AFSOUTH was a stepchild in the command structure: For the large majority of the Allies, the likeliest battleground was to be located in Germany, and consequently, they believed that this is where NATO should concentrate its efforts. This "Central Front Bias" has permeated the Alliance in spite of a strategic reality repeatedly uttered by policymakers and military strategists alike which highlighted the importance of the Mediterranean not only from an economic point of view, but even from a Cold War perspective.

> Should we be forced into a conflict, I believe the Soviets would place the following at the top of their wartime objectives in the Southern region: countering the strike capability of the carrier battle groups; seizing control of the Turkish Straits to permit their Black Sea Fleet unrestricted access to the Mediterranean — which would permit free flow of the economic support they need in the flank, and to prevent the entry of NATO ships into the Black Sea — and interdicting NATO reinforcements and resupply of the southern front.[36]

Continuously neglected by planners, the Southern region was outnumbered toward the end of the Cold War by the Warsaw Pact both in land and air forces. In the Southern region, the Soviet Union and its Allies matched NATO's 41 divisions with 71, and offered 2,450 aircraft against NATO's 1,000. Although the Alliance did have naval superiority, a conflict in this part of the world between the Warsaw Pact and NATO would have given the former a significant advantage — particularly because the Southern region is separated from the rest of the Alliance by the Alps, and reinforcements, therefore, would have taken significant time.[37]

JFC-Naples inherited this partial neglect to some extent. Although in charge of NATO's Operation in Kosovo (KFOR) — its former training mission in Iraq ended in 2011 — and the Mediterranean anti-terrorism mission Operation ACTIVE ENDEAVOUR, JFC-Naples rivaled for strategic attention in particular with JFC-Brunssum which conducted NATO's engagement in Afghanistan, the International Security Assistance Force (ISAF). It was, therefore, not entirely surprising that the headquarters was not as well equipped for the Libya operation as it was supposed to be.

JFC-Naples' mission was to prepare for, plan, and conduct military operations in order to preserve the peace, security, and territorial integrity of Alliance member states and freedom of the seas and economic lifelines throughout SACEUR's Area of Responsibility (AOR) and beyond. But it also was to contribute to crisis management and deterrence by ensuring that assigned headquarters and forces were at the designated state of readiness for the conduct and support of operations, and to conduct prudent operational level military analysis and planning, which includes the identification of required forces.[38]

In contrast to its predecessor AFSOUTH, JFC-Naples did not have an assigned geographic area, but was focusing on a range of operations including peacekeeping and peace enforcement. Since the headquarters was already quite busy with three operations when the Libyan crisis erupted, the capacity to take over OUP could hardly be taken for granted; it required kinetic action rather than peace enforcement, and the region concerned demanded specialist expertise.

The speed with which the mission was taken on meant that staff had to be drafted in from other posi-

14

tions within JFC-Naples while the operational head-quarters were hastily set up in a ballroom. Although in theory NATO's Force Command in Madrid could be relied on to draft the necessary personnel, the speed of the mission, as well as the specific skill requirements, effectively precluded this possibility. As the Alliance's bureaucracy seemed at times to rule out the urgency of military action (partner officers were told computers would not be available in less than 3 months), JFC-Naples was not properly equipped for an actual crisis of this dimension, but managed to improvise on a large scale.

As NATO remodels its command structure, these shortcomings are being partly addressed, and JFC-Naples will grow into a headquarters capable of deploying up to a major joint operation in theater. However, since the uncertainty brought on by the Arab Spring makes instability and violence a likely scenario, the Mediterranean remains an area of concern, where NATO might need capacities for operations ranging from Responsibility to Protect[39] missions to peacekeeping. Manning and equipping the headquarters appropriately would be the logical consequence of this consideration, as would the allocation of a specific area of responsibility.

Lesson 3: Do Not Ignore Culture.

NATO's Libya operation was the Alliance's first combat action against an Arab country; although the Alliance already had an operation in another country in the region, Iraq, this was extremely small (150 troops) and limited to training only. Arguably, individual member states had gathered experience during Operation IRAQI FREEDOM, which, although not a

NATO operation, had included 19 of the then 26 Allies. But, as a collective and in its joint headquarters, NATO engaged for the first time within an Arab strategic environment. In spite of this, the Alliance paid rather limited attention to Libya's cultural terrain and had no cultural advisers on the staff of OUP — not from Libya, nor another Arab country, and not anyone familiar with local conditions. Although there, indeed, were people with limited local knowledge involved in the planning of the campaign, the headquarters in charge of it, JFC-Naples, did not employ cultural advisers. Instead, it occasionally improvised cultural advice from liaison officers from Jordan, Qatar, and the UAE, or NATO officers who had worked in Tripoli as defense attachés for less than a year. This could not make up for the fact that there, indeed, was no understanding of Libya — either its regime or its population. In other words, there was no structured approach to a nation that has been visited and studied all too little for the past 4 decades — although no less than General Sun Tzu had postulated that knowing your enemy is crucial in conflict.

This lack of an approach is partly the result of a general lack of research on Libya. Research activities within the country had been difficult for decades, because the regime not only focused all in-country political research on its ideology laid out in the Green Book, but made life difficult for foreigners attempting to shed light on local conditions. Furthermore, international intelligence activities died down in Libya after 2003, when the regime decided to abandon its nuclear, biological, and chemical weapons program and ceased the support of international terrorism. As Major General Margaret Woodward, the commander of the joint force air component for operation ODYSSEY DAWN, OUP's predecessor, noted:

> There was little 'intelligence preparation' of the area of conflict. . . . The U.S. Intelligence Community hadn't viewed Libya as a potential adversary 'for years'.[40]

The same was true for most other NATO Allies.

This lack of knowledge was not helped by the fact that JFC-Naples did not have a geographical area of focus, and regional expertise therefore did not exist in the headquarters. Although the salary of an analyst represents only a fraction of other operational costs, nations seem to consider analysis of a strategic environment too costly. Yet, understanding of conditions on the ground was of particular relevance in the case of OUP, where situational awareness was restricted by the absence of a land component and limitations of intelligence gathered on the ground.

Although the widespread lack of expertise on Libya was an aspect NATO had to make do with, the way it attempted to fill the gap was not ideal. Relying on the advice of officers from the Gulf states or Jordan, the Alliance replaced a distinctly Libyan culture with a generic Arab one, which watered its specifics distinctly down. As JFC-Naples later recognized, Libya differs vastly in culture from that of the Gulf states; as JFC-Naples sought experts on Libya, it all too often relied on researchers and officers from NATO countries with outdated or limited knowledge. JFC-Naples ultimately attempted to reach out to Libyan researchers located in Libya, but was not able to do so because of the Alliance's rules of engagement, which clearly interdicted direct contact with locals. This aspect was sidestepped when OUP commander General Charles

Bouchard met with president of the rebel body NTC Mustafa Abdel Jalil in his Canadian, not NATO, capacity. Yet, as it turned out, even people on the ground in Libya had a very incomplete picture of the situation that was confused by lack of communication, disinformation, and the fluidity as well as complexity of internal conflict.

The improvised advice OUP relied on turned out to be a failure, as officers involved in the campaign admitted, nobody predicted several of the turns the operation took. Qaddafi's holding on to power, the comparable weakness but surprising resilience and adaptability of the armed forces, and apparent passivity shown by the population of Tripoli, whose uprising was expected, were all features of a terrain widely misunderstood. Given that the ground component was crucial to the mission's success, cultural advice would have made an important contribution to the general understanding of the situation within Libya as the operation evolved.

While NATO continues to deal with nations and cultures very different from those of Europe or North America, it is rather slow in acknowledging the importance of having an accurate grasp of local conditions outside the purely military field. The success eventually achieved by OUP should not lead to the conclusion that cultural advisers are unnecessary. What must really be asked is whether success could have come earlier with a thorough understanding of local circumstances — e.g., in anticipating rebel and civilian population behavior, be it in Tripoli or Misrata, on the basis of sound judgment rather than speculation.

Lesson 4: Close the Politico-Military Gap.

In many ways, OUP was "the war that wasn't." As the legal interpretations of UNSC Resolution 1973 made clear, the operation did not seek to topple Colonel Qaddafi's regime, let alone assassinate him. Its declared aim was solely the protection of civilians in a situation of internal conflict, and, therefore, it conformed to the norm of "Responsibility to Protect." Yet, against the backdrop of international political pressure, the Alliance's neutrality and agenda quickly became a point of discussion. As military personnel bemoaned, the resolution did not lend itself to military planning: the protection of civilians does not indicate an end state to be achieved, nor does it identify an enemy. For a mission to be planned and executed properly, its outline needs to be more precise. As the translation of the resolution's wording into military action required more specification, concrete indications needed to be found that would point to effectively protected civilians. After consultation, it was agreed that the mission would have achieved its objective when: a) all attacks and threats of attack against civilians and civilian-populated areas have ended; b) the regime has verifiably withdrawn to bases all military forces, including snipers, mercenaries, and other paramilitary forces, including from all populated areas they have forcibly entered, occupied, or besieged throughout all of Libya; and, c) the regime has permitted immediate, full, safe, and unhindered humanitarian access to all the people in Libya in need of assistance.[41]

Yet, the disconnect between military planning and political reasoning continued throughout the operation. As the military rules of engagement of NATO very clearly excluded any regime change as a mission objective, political pressure mounted to remove Colonel Qaddafi from power. The Contact Group, a merger of representatives from 21 countries and representatives from the UN, the Arab League, NATO, the European Union (EU), the Organization of Islamic Conference, and the Cooperation Council for the Arab Gulf States, took a firm stance at its meeting in early-April 2011, declaring that "Qaddafi and his regime had lost all legitimacy and he must leave power . . . Qaddafi's continued presence would threaten any resolution of the crisis."[42] At the Berlin meeting of NATO's Foreign Ministers with those nations participating in OUP in April 2011, not even 2 weeks into the operation, the group "strongly" endorsed the Contact Group's call for Qaddafi to leave power.[43] The impression that NATO's operation was really about changing the Libyan regime hence solidified, regardless of the fact that JFC-Naples continued to interpret UNSC Resolution 1973 strictly in terms of providing civilian protection. In a joint article, U.S. President Obama, France's President Nicholas Sarkozy, and Great Britain's Prime Minister David Cameron explained that:

> [O]ur duty and our mandate under U.N. Security Council Resolution 1973 is to protect civilians, and we are doing that. It is not to remove Gadhafi by force. But it is impossible to imagine a future for Libya with Gadhafi in power. . . . It is unthinkable that someone who has tried to massacre his own people can play a part in their future government . . . so long as Gadhafi is in power, NATO and its coalition partners must maintain their operations so that civilians remain protected and the pressure on the regime builds.[44]

The call for regime change was reiterated at the Libya Contact Group's second meeting in May, further supported by a declaration by NATO's Secretary General Anders Fogh Rasmussen, which echoed the regime's loss of legitimacy:

> I am confident that combination of strong military pressure and increased political pressure and support for the opposition will eventually lead to the collapse of the regime.[45]

Yet, this stood in stark contrast to the military interpretations of UNSC Resolution 1973. As pressure mounted throughout the summer of 2011, OUP commander General Charles Bouchard had to explain that his orders were "not regime change or to kill a head of state."[46]

But the clear discrepancy between the political and the military level, the legitimacy of UNSC Resolution 1973, and the political ambition, as well as between NATO as a collective and its individual member states, confused the public in Allied and non-Allied countries. The same was true of the legal distinction between Allied and national caveats. As General Bouchard was not allowed to have direct contacts with the rebels, he encountered the head of the NTC in his Canadian capacity, and Qatar sent ground forces into Libya outside of OUP.[47] Yet, in the public perception, this legal distinction is not necessarily clear and contributes to confusion between NATO as a collective and its individual members or partner nations.

The unclear distinction between NATO's military action solely for the purpose of civilian protection and political declarations on the member-state level calling for regime change particularly upset Russia and China. They had acquiesced to UNSC Resolution 1973 only because it was precisely not about regime change — thereby reviving the international debate opposing national sovereignty to the protection of human rights. Political capital was thus squandered by the inconsistency between the political and military levels. In practice, this meant that the political problem was passed on to the military level, where it did not belong.

Lesson 5: Improve Strategic Communication.

Although strategic communication is not an entirely new idea, the Alliance recognized the necessity for an overall concept during the NATO-led operation International Security Assistance Force (ISAF) in Afghanistan, when rallying the Afghan people's support for the mission's objectives turned out to be more difficult than anticipated. In 2009, only 2 years before the crisis in Libya erupted, NATO issued its first strategic communications concept, which aimed at supporting an operation's objectives by ensuring that audiences receive clear, fair, and opportune information regarding actions and that the interpretation of the Alliance's messages are not left solely to NATO's adversaries or other audiences.[48]

Actors of strategic communication are psychological operations (PYSOPS) departments, public diplomacy, and media relations units — essentially, any unit involved in the operation that reaches out and communicates with a broader audience crucial to the mission's success. Target audiences can be primary as well as collateral; messaging can shift, depending on events and perceptions, and therefore needs to be highly adaptable. In particular, the strategic communication efforts of antagonists need to be taken into account.

In the case of OUP, NATO's first strategic communication efforts targeted the Libyan population, which can be clustered roughly in two separate groups: on the one hand, the civilian population; on the other, members of the regime's forces. The civilian population needed to be favorable to NATO's efforts; avoiding civilian casualties was therefore not only a moral imperative but also a strategic one, as civilian support would most certainly wane with increasing numbers of casualties. Leaflets dropped by the Alliance warned civilians hours before the air strikes: "Warning: Step away from military activities." In addition, NATO dropped leaflets informing Libyans about a hot line Libyans could call to pass on information they deemed useful and a radio station designed to warn civilians in time. As the UN noted, NATO "conducted a highly precise campaign with a demonstrable determination to avoid civilian casualties."[49]

Nevertheless, criticism on the Alliance's methods emerged shortly after the mission's inception. The League of Arab States' Secretary General bemoaned the amplitude of the campaign:

> What is happening in Libya differs from the aim of imposing a no-fly zone. And what we want is the protection of civilians and not the shelling of more civilians.[50]

Although successive investigations by different bodies after the end of the campaign showed that 40-70 civilians died as a result of NATO air strikes,[51] the fact that the Alliance did not confirm any responsibility for these casualties has only fueled speculations—

reports in the Arab as well as the Russian media spoke of 700-1,000 civilians killed by NATO air strikes.[52] Although the Alliance's reasoning for not investigating in Libya proper is sound and its cooperation with the investigating UN body was extensive, it has backfired in strategic communication terms, since it was still interpreted as NATO avoiding its responsibilities.

NATO's strategic communication efforts also targeted another part of Libyan society, namely, the regime's forces. Encouraging desertion of both Libyan fighters and mercenaries, the leaflets dropped in Arabic contained messages such as:

> Officers, soldiers and regime fighters of great Libya: Many Senior officers have already defected and followed their conscience. Stop being part of the fighting. Return to your family and serve your country by laying down your weapons, leaving your post and respecting the right of all Libyans to live in peace.

Others used a more threatening tone:

> You are no match for NATO's superior weapons systems and air power. Continuing to man your posts and equipment will result in your death.

Another set appealed to the professionalism of the soldiers: "Professional soldiers don't attack civilians. Do not bring dishonor to yourselves and to your families." Lastly, a number of leaflets sought to criminalize Qaddafi and erode support for him:

> Gadhafi has been indicted by the International Criminal Court. Will you share a prison cell with him? Who will support your family? Make a choice before it is too late.

The pictures used on these leaflets showed Libyan resistance fighter Omar Mokhtar, juxtaposing him to a speech balloon asking Qaddafi, "Why do you allow our Libyan brothers to fight and kill each other?" To what extent these leaflets encouraged the disintegration and desertion of the Libyan forces is difficult to measure; although the Libyan forces suffered significant desertion, the direct correlation with NATO leaflets is hard to establish.

In addition, the general public in Allied and Arab countries as well as in Russia developed collaborative strategic communication audiences. This was particularly the case, as the media began to question the true motive behind the mandate for regime change, accused France and the UK of exceeding the mandate, and created in summer 2011 the "stalemate narrative" — the notion that the Alliance was not achieving its goals. The pan-Arab daily *Al-Quds al-Arabi* wrote in June 2011:

> It is obvious that, by targeting residential buildings, NATO seeks to assassinate and physically liquidate the Libyan leader. . . . UN Security Council Resolution 1973 does not provide for the assassination of the Libyan leader or the overthrow of the ruling regime.[53]

Another pan-Arab daily, *Al-Hayat*, noted that:

> NATO is looking for political and legal pretexts to prolong the war in order to be able to get an explicit UN resolution to allow the occupation of Libya in the same way as that of Iraq.[54]

NATO attempted to turn this around by relentlessly repeating the content of UNSC Resolution 1973 and the military interpretations of it as well as the complexity of the Libyan crisis on the ground, both in press conferences and an especially set-up YouTube Channel in Arabic.

Nevertheless, the Libyan regime's strategic communication proved to be comparatively resilient and creative. It not only succeeded in recruiting a public relations firm for this purpose, but managed to escort BBC journalists into a hospital, showing corpses of young children supposedly killed in NATO air strikes. Tapping into traditional Arab grievances, Qaddafi used words such as "colonialism" and "imperialism," called the rebels "NATO agents," and promised to exterminate them like rats.

Although there *was* Arab support for the NATO operation, news coverage remained neutral to negative, depending on the region, and proved volatile throughout the conflict. Al-Jazeera, a channel the Alliance has quarreled with in the past over Afghanistan, defended the operation prominently and helped strengthen Arab support, but others remained critical of the number of civilian deaths. As a result, NATO's traditionally rather negative image in the region has not yet changed; the long-term impact of OUP in this respect will depend to a large extent on internal Libyan developments. Although the Alliance's contribution very likely saved a large number of civilian lives, the role it played in this respect might well be obscured by other, negative, developments.

Overall, the strategic communication of the regime forces (and of the NTC as well) was better attuned to the local sentiment of target audiences and thus to the most relevant media profile. The extremely rapid creation of rebel TV station Libya Ahrar ("Free Libya") reflects a constantly growing agility and adaptability in strategic communication. NATO has to adapt to this sooner rather than later.

Lesson 6: The Aftermath of Intervention.

NATO's Libya operation aimed at protecting civilians in a situation of internal strife. In a conflict opposing the regime and rebel forces, the Alliance nominally never took sides — although its action de facto tipped the balance, which had been in favor of the regime. Once the regime of Colonel Qaddafi had been toppled and Libya's "liberation" proclaimed on October 23, 2011, the Alliance brought OUP to an end a week later despite calls from the Libyan NTC to maintain NATO air patrolling:

> We hope (NATO) will continue its campaign until at least the end of this year to serve us and neighboring countries, ensuring that no arms are infiltrated into those countries and to ensure the security of Libyans from some remnants of Qaddafi's forces who have fled to nearby countries.[55]

Yet, in the immediate aftermath of the regime's fall, the transitional council sent mixed messages on the acceptability of international support in security terms.

Although calling on NATO and hinting at possible requests from Arab states to assist Libya in the immediate aftermath of the end of the conflict, the NTC also firmly rejected any military personnel on the ground, even UN observers.[56] As the regime's security forces had virtually imploded, Libya's security therefore fell into the hands of the multiple militias, which continued to proliferate after the conflict ended. In a situation of effective lawlessness, Libyans protested several times against the militia rule and asked for their disbandment. However, militia leaders refused disbandment as long as no military or police force could take over.[57]

While the country prepared its first elections in half a century, vetted candidates, and sought to bring its oil industry back on track, security sector reconstruction advanced rather slowly. Throughout the first half of 2012, attacks on the Red Cross's offices in Tripoli and Benghazi, the Tunisian Consulate, and the convoy of the British ambassador, and a brief occupation of Tripoli Airport as a result of intermilitia fights indicated a progressive implosion of Libya's security, which culminated in an attack on the U.S. Consulate in Benghazi—resulting in the death of four embassy staff, including the ambassador.[58] Without a doubt, Libya's ongoing security challenge will influence the way future interventions in internal strife will be conducted. If the government is unable to take back control of the security sector, Libya might very well be headed to a failed-state scenario—which, of course, would cast a shadow on NATO's operation as well.

CONCLUSION

Albeit hailed by NATO's Supreme Allied Commander Europe, Admiral James Stavridis, as a "model intervention,"[59] the Alliance can still learn a number of strategic lessons from its Libyan adventure. These include, of course, technical elements such as air power and command structure, but extends to aspects such as culture, strategic communication, and the general political backdrop against which OUP was conducted. Most importantly, OUP will relaunch the Alliance's debate on its collective stance on the Middle East. After all, it proved to be a moment of division for NATO as well as Germany, which abstained from the vote on UNSC Resolution 1973; only six NATO Allies actively participated in the operation.

In spite of their two partnership programs, the Mediterranean Dialogue and the Istanbul Cooperation Initiative, the Allies have so far held very different visions of how to deal with the region. This is, in part, a leftover from the Alliance's first 4 decades, when the Mediterranean and its Southern rim hardly featured outside the Cold War context, and, in part, an outcome of different analysis over which regions should matter to the Alliance beyond the Soviet threat. Depending on geographical location, the Allies would emphasize the Central, the Northern, or the Southern Front.

Mostly, however, this lack of vision reflects a strong preference of individual Allies for bi- or tri-lateralism when dealing with this part of the world. As a region of international importance, not only because of large petrol resources but also the existence of maritime choke points and one of the most important world trade routes, it attracts those Allies with strategic interests that might threaten NATO consensus. Yet, if the Alliance wants to continue to reach out into its Southern neighbor area, a common vision will be necessary to achieve that goal.

The euphoria over the end of a brutal regime that lasted 4 decades in Libya should not disguise the fact that the consequences of OUP are not yet fully visible. Indeed, a number of lessons to be learned will possibly emerge only several years after the end of OUP. It would be a mistake to think that NATO's Libya adventure ended with the drawdown of the military mission; whether the Alliance likes it or not, its reputation is at stake in Libya's long reconstruction process.

ENDNOTES

1. "Muammar Gaddafi Condemns Tunisia Uprising," *The Guardian*, January 16, 2011, available from *www.guardian.co.uk/world/2011/jan/16/muammar-gaddafi-condemns-tunisia-uprising*.

2. "Libyan Protestors Clash with Police in Benghazi," *The Guardian*, February 16, 2011, available from *www.guardian.co.uk/world/2011/feb/16/libyan-protesters-clash-with-police*.

3. "Libya on Brink as Protests Hit Tripoli," *The Guardian*, February 21, 2011, available from *www.guardian.co.uk/world/2011/feb/20/libya-defiant-protesters-feared-dead*.

4. "Raging Gaddafi Orders Forces to 'Capture the Rats,' " ABC News, February 23, 2011, available from *www.abc.net.au/news/2011-02-23/raging-gaddafi-orders-forces-to-capture-the-rats/1953788*.

5. "Libyan Leader Should Stand Down as He Has 'Lost Legitimately,' "Obama," *The Guardian*, March 3, 2011, available from *www.guardian.co.uk/world/2011/mar/03/libyan-leader-stand-down-obama*.

6. "Rebel Leader Calls for 'Immediate Action' on No-fly Zone," CNN, March 10, 2011, available from *edition.cnn.com/2011/WORLD/africa/03/09/libya.civil.war/index.html*.

7. "Arab League Backs Libya No-fly Zone," BBC News, March 12, 2011, available from *www.bbc.co.uk/news/world-africa-12723554*.

8. "Gaddafi Tells Rebel City, Benghazi, 'We Will Show No Mercy'," *The Huffington Post*, March 17, 2011, available from *www.huffingtonpost.com/2011/03/17/gaddafi-benghazi-libya-news_n_837245.html*.

9. "Security Council Approves 'No-Fly Zone' over Libya, Authorizing 'All Necessary Measures' to Protect Civilians, by Vote of 10 in Favour with 5 Abstentions," United Nations, March 17, 2011, available from *www.un.org/News/Press/docs/2011/sc10200.doc.htm*.

10. "NATO Secretary General's Statement on Libya No-fly Zone," NATO, March 24, 2011, available from *www.nato.int/cps/en/natolive/news_71763.htm.*

11. Sorties in general are military deployments with a specific mission; strike sorties are intended to identify and engage appropriate targets, but need not always involve deployment of ammunition.

12. "Accidental Heroes: Britain, France and the Libya Operation," London, UK: Royal United Services Institute (RUSI), September 2011, available from *www.rusi.org/downloads/assets/RUSI-InterimLibyaReport.pdf.*

13. UNSC Resolution 1973, March 17, 2011, available from *www.un.org/Docs/sc/unsc_resolutions11.htm.*

14. "United States Activities in Libya," Washington, DC: The White House, June 15, 2011, p. 25, available from *www.washingtonpost.com/wp-srv/politics/documents/united-states-activities-libya.html.*

15. "Gates Warns of Risks of a No-fly Zone," *The New York Times*, March 2, 2011, available from *www.nytimes.com/2011/03/03/world/africa/03military.html?pagewanted=all.*

16. "Libyan Air Defenses Would Fade Fast," *Aviation Week*, March 8, 2011, available from *www.aviationweek.com/Blogs.aspx?plckBlogId=Blog:27ec4a53-dcc8-42d0-bd3a-01329aef79a7&plckController=Blog&plckBlogPage=BlogViewPost&newspaperUserId=27ec4a53-dcc8-42d0-bd3a-01329aef79a7&plckPostId=Blog%253A27ec4a53-dcc8-42d0-bd3a-01329aef79a7Post%253Ab5d2af1a-9b89-40d6-acb6-ee7a623098a0&plckScript=blogScript&plckElementId=blogDest.*

17. "1986: US Launches Air Strikes on Libya," BBC News, April 15, 1986, available from *news.bbc.co.uk/onthisday/hi/dates/stories/april/15/newsid_3975000/3975455.stm.*

18. Jeremiah Gertler, "Operation Odyssey Dawn (Libya): Background and Issues for Congress," March 30, 2011, p. 10, available from *www.fas.org/sgp/crs/natsec/R41725.pdf.*

19. "Libya No-Fly Zone Would Require NATO Military Action, General Says," ABC News, March 1, 2011, available from *abcnews.go.com/Politics/libya-fly-zone-require-nato-military-force/story?id=13031952#.UEeAE7VcAcs*.

20. Department of Defense (DoD) News Briefing with Admiral Locklear via Telephone from USS *Mount Whitney*, Washington, DC: U.S. Department of Defense, March 22, 2011, available from *www.defense.gov/transcripts/transcript.aspx?transcriptid=4793*.

21. "Libyan Rebels near Ajdabiya 'Killed in NATO Air Strike'," BBC News, April 7, 2011, available from *www.bbc.co.uk/news/world-africa-12997181*; "Libyan Opposition Says NATO Strike Hit Rebel Fighters; 13 Killed," CNN, March 3, 2011, available from *edition.cnn.com/2011/WORLD/africa/04/02/libya.war/index.html*; "NATO says its aircraft hit Libyan rebel column," *Reuters*, June 18, 2011, available from *www.reuters.com/article/2011/06/18/us-libya-nato-rebel-idUSTRE75H22120110618*.

22. "Libye: point de situation n°50 — bilan de l'operation Unified Protector' ("Libya: Update Number 50: Balance of Operation Unified Protector"), November 8, 2011, Ministere de la Defense Francais, available from *www.defense.gouv.fr/operations/autres-operations/operation-harmattan-libye/actualites/libye-point-de-situation-n-50-bilan-de-l-operation-unified-protector*; "NATO Operations in Libya: Data Journalism Breaks Down Which Country Does What," *The Guardian*, October 31, 2011, available from *www.guardian.co.uk/news/datablog/2011/may/22/nato-libya-data-journalism-operations-country#*.

23. See also Grant T. Hammond, "Myths of the Air War over Serbia: Some 'Lessons' Not to Learn," *Aerospace Power Journal*, Winter 2000, available from *www.airpower.au.af.mil/airchronicles/apj/apj00/win00/hammond.htm*.

24. Author interview with representative of the Warrior Affairs Commission, Tripoli, Lebanon, June 2012.

25. "At Least 30,000 Killed, 50,000 Wounded in Libyan Conflict," *The Tripoli Post*, September 8, 2011, available from *www.tripolipost.com/articledetail.asp?c=1&i=6862&archive=1*.

26. "Distribution of Warriors According to Age Group and Educational Level," Tripoli, Lebanon: Warrior Affairs Commission, June 2012.

27. UNSC Resolution 1973.

28. Final Report of the Panel of Experts Established Pursuant to Security Council Resolution 1973 (2011) Concerning Libya, UN Security Council, March 20, 2012, pp. 20-22, available from *www.un.org/ga/search/view_doc.asp?symbol=S/2012/163*.

29. "Al-Jazeera Footage Captures 'Western Troops on the Ground' in Libya," *The Guardian*, May 30, 2011, available from *www.guardian.co.uk/world/2011/may/30/western-troops-on-ground-libya*; "Foreign Forces in Libya Helping Rebel Forces Advance," CNN, August 24, 2011, available from *articles.cnn.com/2011-08-24/world/libya.foreign.forces_1_rebel-forces-special-forces-rebel-units?_s=PM:WORLD*.

30. Final Report of the Panel of Experts Established Pursuant to Security Council Resolution 1973 (2011) Concerning Libya, p. 23.

31. *Ibid.*, p. 25.

32. "Qatar Admits Sending Hundreds of Troops to Support Libya Rebels," *The Guardian*, October 26, 2011, available from *www.guardian.co.uk/world/2011/oct/26/qatar-troops-libya-rebels-support*.

33. "Qatar Admits It Had Boots on the Ground in Libya, NTC Seeks further NATO Help," *Al-Arabiya*, October 26, 2011, available from *www.alarabiya.net/articles/2011/10/26/173833.html*.

34. W. Bruce Weinrod and Charles L. Barry, "NATO Command Structure: Considerations for the Future," Washington, DC: Center for Technology and National Security Policy, National Defense University, September 2010, p. 8, available from *www.ndu.edu/CTNSP/docUploaded/DTP%2075%20NATO%20Command%20Structure.pdf*.

35. Letter from General Dwight D. Eisenhower to Admiral Robert Carney, first CINCSOUTH, quoted in AFSOUTH Public Information, *AFSOUTH at 50: Defending Peace, Fostering Stability,* Naples, Italy: Alfredo Guida Editore, 2001, p. 26.

36. James Busey, "The Lion's Share: The Challenge for Allied Forces Southern Europe," *NATO's Sixteen Nations,* July/August 1988, Vol. 32, No. 4, p. 19.

37. *Ibid.,* pp. 18-25.

38. "JFC Naples Mission," Allied Joint Force Command Naples, available from *www.jfcnaples.nato.int/page87211118.aspx.*

39. Responsibility to Protect: a United Nations concept designed to prevent genocide, war crimes, crimes against humanity, and ethnic cleansing.

40. John A. Tirpak, "Lessons From Libya," *Air Force Magazine,* December 2011, p. 36.

41. NATO: Statement on Libya, April 14, 2011, available from *www.nato.int/cps/en/natolive/official_texts_72544.htm.*

42. "Libya Contact Group: Chair's Statement," London, UK: Foreign and Commonwealth Office, April 13, 2011, available from *www.fco.gov.uk/en/news/latest-news/?id=583592582&view=News.*

43. NATO: Statement on Libya, April 14, 2011, available from *www.nato.int/cps/en/natolive/official_texts_72544.htm.*

44. "Libya Letter by Obama, Cameron and Sarkozy," *The Daily Star* (Lebanon), April 15, 2011, available from *www.dailystar. com.lb/News/Middle-East/Apr/15/Libya-letter-by-Obama-Cameron-and-Sarkozy-Full-text.ashx#axzz27P0aaGZE.*

45. "NATO: Gaddafi Forces 'Significantly Degraded,'" Al Jazeera, May 20, 2011, available from *www.aljazeera.com/news/ africa/2011/05/201151914159509484.html.*

46. "Libya Conflict: NATO's Man against Gaddafi," BBC News, June 26, 2011, available from *www.bbc.co.uk/news/world-europe-13919380.*

47. "Qatar Admits It Had Boots on the Ground in Libya; NTC Seeks Further NATO Help," *Al-Arabiya*, October 26, 2011, available from *www.alarabiya.net/articles/2011/10/26/173833.html*.

48. Anaïs Reding *et al.*, *NATO's Strategic Communications Concept and its Relevance for France*, Santa Monica, CA: Rand Corporation: 2010, p. 4, available from *www.rand.org/content/dam/rand/pubs/technical_reports/2010/RAND_TR855.2.pdf*.

49. Report of the International Commission of Inquiry on Libya, New York: UN Human Rights Council, March 2, 2012, p. 2.

50. "Arab League Condemns Broad Western Bombing Campaigns in Libya," *The Washington Post*, March 20, 2011, available from *www.washingtonpost.com/world/arab-league-condemns-broad-bombing-campaign-in-libya/2011/03/20/AB1pSg1_story.html*.

51. "HRW Urges NATO to Probe Libyan Civilians' Deaths, but Libya Says No Need to Investigate," *Al Arabiya News,* December 16, 2011, available from *www.alarabiya.net/articles/2011/12/16/182835.html*; Report of the International Commission of Inquiry on Libya, p. 17; "Libya: The Forgotten Victims of NATO Air Strikes," Amnesty International, March 2012, available from *www.amnesty.org/en/library/asset/MDE19/003/2012/en/8982a094-60ff-4783-8aa8-8c80a4fd0b14/mde190032012en.pdf*; "In Strikes on Libya by NATO, an Unspoken Civilian Toll," *The New York Times*, December 17, 2011, available from *www.nytimes.com/2011/12/18/world/africa/scores-of-unintended-casualties-in-nato-war-in-libya.html?ref=opinion*.

52. "Civilian Cost of NATO victory in Libya," *Russia Today*, October 20, 2011, available from *rt.com/news/libya-nato-civilian-deaths-323/*; "Libya Says NATO Strikes Kill(?) 19 Civilians," *Al-Jazeera*, June 21, 2011, available from *www.aljazeera.com/news/africa/2011/06/2011620214646273991.html*.

53. BBC Monitoring, "Pan-Arab Daily Criticizes NATO for Targeting 'Residential Buildings' in Libya," June 21, 2011.

54. BBC Monitoring, "Writer Criticizes NATO's Role in Libya; Calls for Redrafting UN Resolution," April 21, 2011.

55. "Qatar Admits It Had Boots on the Ground in Libya."

56. "Libya's Interim Leaders Reject UN Military Personnel," *BBC News*, August 31, 2011, available from *www.bbc.co.uk/news/world-africa-14726292*.

57. "Can Libya's Armed Groups be Disbanded?" *Al-Jazeera*, January 8, 2012, available from *www.aljazeera.com/programmes/insidestory/2012/01/2012156215196506.html*.

58. "Chris Stevens, US Ambassador to Libya, killed in Benghazi Attack," *The Guardian*, September 12, 2012, available from *www.guardian.co.uk/world/2012/sep/12/chris-stevens-us-ambassador-libya-killed*.

59. Ivo H. Daalder and James G. Stavridis, "NATO's Victory in Libya: The Right Way to Run an Intervention," *Foreign Affairs*, March/April 2012, p. 2, available from *aco.nato.int/resources/site631/saceur/documents/Daalder_Stavridis_final.pdf*.

www.ingramcontent.com/pod-product-compliance
Lightning Source LLC
Chambersburg PA
CBHW070239290526
45789CB00004B/1690